Ten Key Teachings from Paul's Letters

Bible Basics for Adults

by Philip and Randi Quanbeck

Leader Guide

Augsburg Fortress, Minneapolis

Contents

BIBLE BASICS FOR ADULTS
Ten Key Teachings from Paul's Letters Leader Guide
This leader guide has a corresponding learner book.

Editors: Katherine A. Evensen and Rich Gordon
Designer: Craig P. Claeys
Illustrator: Parrot Graphics/Patti Isaacs

ISBN 0-8066-3635-1

Manufactured in U.S.A.

1 2 3 4 5 6 7 8 9 0 1 2 3 4 5 6 7 8 9

Cover photo: © Lars Hansen Photography

Overview

FEWER AND FEWER ADULTS feel comfortable studying the Bible alone or with others. **Bible Basics for Adults** resources address the needs of adults who do not know basic Bible stories and the importance of the Bible to daily Christian living. These six courses will make it easy for adults who know little about the Bible to study the Bible.

The courses are designed for adult learners who may feel intimidated to study the Bible and are curious as to how—or if—the Bible is important to their lives. These six courses will help adults become comfortable studying the Bible for a lifetime.

General Objectives

The objectives of these courses are to help learners who are not familiar with the Bible and its stories to:
- gain familiarity with the Bible;
- see the Bible as important to their lives;
- gain confidence in using the Bible for their growth in faith and life;
- see their life stories—their joys, sorrows, relationships, and search for meaning—as part of the larger narrative of the people of God that is presented in the Bible.

Course Descriptions

The six courses and their descriptions are as follows:

1. Ten Key Events in Jesus' Life. This course helps adult learners who are unfamiliar with the Bible to gain a basic understanding of the biblical stories of the life and ministry of Jesus.

2. Ten Key People from the Bible. This course introduces adults to central stories of important biblical characters. In this course, adult learners not only enjoy the study of the Bible through stories, but see in those accounts questions and issues that connect with their own lives and journey of faith today.

3. Ten Key Events from the Bible. This course helps people understand that God is active in history and in the lives of God's people. This study identifies the life, death, and resurrection of Jesus as the pivotal event of history and the source of our meaning and hope.

4. Ten Key Passages from the Bible. This course presents biblical themes that are central to the Christian faith. Through this study participants will celebrate the Christian message in both the Old and New Testament. Participants will have their daily lives and faith strengthened by the Word of God.

5. Ten Key Teachings from Paul's Letters. This course helps learners understand that God is active in individuals' lives and the Christian communities to which they belong. This study identifies the life, death, and resurrection of Jesus Christ as central to our identity, providing meaning and hope.

6. Ten Key Promises from the Bible. This course helps people understand that God is faithful and trustworthy throughout the generations. God's promises culminate in Jesus Christ, who brings forgiveness and life to all people.

Using the Leader Guide

LEADERS of the **Bible Basics for Adults** courses will discover a helpful new approach awaiting them as they explore each leader guide. Leaders will teach from a two-page session plan designed to allow easy access to ideas for each segment of class time.

Introductions. Each leader guide begins with these introductory resources:
- a description of the adult learner;

- help in using the leader guide to integrate the learners' life experiences in basic Bible study;
- a course introduction.

Session plans. Each two-page session plan begins with a "Theme Statement" that highlights a basic biblical concept shared by the session's two biblical texts.

The first five session plans follow this format:
- **Gathering.** An idea for community building and introducing the session theme;

- **Read the Story.** A strategy for reading the first Bible text of the session;
- **Expand the Story.** Ways to discover what the text says about God, the people of God, and the learners;
- **Read the Story.** A strategy for reading the second Bible text of the session;
- **Expand the Story.** Ways to discover what the text says about God, the people of God, and the learners;
- **Focus the Stories.** Activities that focus on the connections learners are able to make between their lives and the two featured Bible texts.

The sixth session plan follows a similar format but focuses on one biblical text. Leaders will choose activities from each part of the session that best meet the needs of the learners. To prepare for an activity listed on a session plan, a leader may be directed to another page in the guide for the following helps:

Discussion strategies. Ways to involve all learners in actively identifying, sharing, and scrutinizing their opinions and life experiences.

Reproducible pages. Ways to expand, not replace, the activities in the learner book. These include process helps that the learner book cannot accomodate. They are referred to in specific session plans and need to be reproduced before the session for use during or after each session.

Common Resources

All six Bible Basics for Adults courses contain a number of pages that can be copied, distributed, and discussed throughout any of the courses. Or this material may be copied and distributed for the learners' reading enjoyment.

LEARNER BOOK
- **How the Bible is Organized (page 23).** This reproducible page gives a simple outline of the books of the Bible. Copies of this outline may be distributed to learners at the beginning of the course to help them identify Old and New Testament books and to locate biblical texts more easily for reading and study.
- **Time Line (pages 24-25).** The time line helps learners put the Bible texts they are studying in each course into the larger context of God's salvation story as documented by Scripture. As you begin the study of each text, refer the learners to the time line to help them appreciate the scope and sequence of God at work in the lives of God's people.

- **How to Read the Bible (page 26).** This page provides three tools for beginning Bible readers. "Finding a Bible Reference" shows learners how to interpret a reference and then track down the passage in the Bible. "Going Deeper" provides questions to help learners dig into and apply a text. Bible readers who want to keep notes in their Bibles about their discoveries and questions will find "Marking Your Bible" useful.
- **Glossary (inside back cover).** The glossary in each course defines key words and phrases in that course, and it is placed in the learner book so it is always available to learners. Note that glossary entries pertinent to each session are identified in a prominent place on each session plan in this guide. Make sure learners understand these words and phrases before the end of each session.

LEADER GUIDE
- **Bible Study Resources (page 26).** All of us have questions about what we read in the Bible. This reproducible page provides a brief description of the various types of references, including the study Bible, cross-reference, commentary, handbook, dictionary, and atlas. Particularly helpful is the explanation of how to use a concordance.
- **Bible Bookmarks (page 27).** Copy this reproducible page and cut out markers to help give learners quick access to the key texts being studied. They can also be used for reflection and prayer at various times between sessions. This serves as a way to connect biblical learning with one's daily life. During the first session, explore with the learners how these bookmarks can be used.
- **Old and New Testament Maps (pages 28-29).** These reproducible maps help learners find important biblical locations in relationship to the Middle East today. Old and New Testament sites are identified on page 29. Make copies of these maps for each learner and refer to the maps at appropriate times during the sessions.
- **The Bible in Worship (page 30).** The Bible is at the center of Christian worship. From the Bible comes much of the content and the general form of our worship. This reproducible page discusses liturgy as the pattern of Bible texts we hear, sing, and pray in worship.
- **Using These Resources in Other Settings (page 31).** Because of the diverse schedules and interests of adult learners, other ways to use this resource are explored. Consider using these other settings as ways to reach more people with this and other Bible studies.

About the Learner

THESE RESOURCES ARE DESIGNED for adults who have an interest in learning basic Bible stories and exploring the importance of the Bible in daily Christian living. Researchers suggest that three-quarters of adults in the church do not participate in Bible study. Add to this the number of adults joining churches and the potential audience for basic Bible study is tremendous. Providing the opportunity to help adult learners become familiar with Bible stories, to gain confidence in their ability to read and understand Scripture, to grow in faith, and to address the issues they face in their lives is a priority for church education leaders.

Getting Started

Adults choose to participate in Bible study groups for a variety of reasons. Research indicates that the following are important factors to consider as you establish Bible study groups in your church.

Adults participate when they believe the experience will help them grow in a way that will benefit them, their families, and their communities. Adults are motivated to finds ways to "make life work" as they face the challenges of daily living. Issues that arise from relationships, family, aging, job transitions, money, and others as defined by the learners need to be addressed in Bible study groups.

Adults participate when they are sure they will not be embarrassed by their lack of biblical knowledge or insight. Many Bible study resources and leaders assume a level of familiarity with the Bible and biblical scholarship that most adults find overwhelming and disconnected with the issues of daily life. Walter Wink, a professor of biblical interpretation, suggests that adults seek insight and not just information. It is the intersection of the biblical text with the experience of the learner that evokes insight. Because we are all experts when it comes to our own experience, no one should be made to feel inadequate when it comes to studying the Bible. (Walter Wink, *Transforming Bible Study: A Leader's Guide,* 2nd ed. [Nashville, Tenn.: Abingdon Press, 1989], 37-38.)

Adults participate when they are comfortable with the other learners in the group. Adults know that they will benefit from the opportunity to see and hear what life looks like from the perspective of others. They know that learning comes from asking, sharing, doing, and imagining. But the idea of sharing personal information with strangers can be a barrier to participation. Learners who have not participated in Bible study as adults are more likely to accept an invitation to join a group of people they know or who have similar concerns (for example, parents with teenagers) than they are to sign up for a group in response to an announcement in a bulletin or newsletter.

Adults participate when the time commitment honors their priorities. Finding a time to meet can be a difficult hurdle to overcome. Parents with young children may appreciate a group that meets every other Monday night rather than weekly. This allows them to be with their children and helps with finding child care. A group of older adults may prefer to meet during the day so they do not have to travel at night.

Recruiting

Keep the following suggestions in mind as you establish groups for basic Bible study:

Keep the groups small. This study focuses on the intersection between basic Bible texts and the learner's life experience. A group of 6 to 10 participants allows for a balance of individual reflection and group discussion that is important in this study.

Start with the groups that already exist in your church (parents with young children, new members, empty nesters, Sunday school teachers, young adults, and so on). People who share concerns and situations in life will be more comfortable together and may have similar schedules.

Make personal invitations. Announcements during worship, in bulletins or newsletters, and community papers are important. But many more adults will respond to a personal invitation to participate in a Bible study group. Make sure they know the details of the study, who else will be there, and the expectations of the participants.

Consider allowing the group to decide on the time and meeting place for the study.

Communicate clearly that this is a study for adults who are interested in learning basic Bible stories and exploring the importance of the Bible in daily Christian living. It is important for this audience to know that you respect their experience in life, their ability to read and understand Bible stories, and their interest in making a positive difference in their lives. It is also important for them to know that you do not expect them to be biblical scholars.

Working with the Adult Learner

Adult learners bring a variety of learning styles, experiences, gifts, and questions to the Bible study. Everyone in the group, both learners and leader, has something to offer to other individuals and to the group. It is important for the leader to recognize and respect the diversity of experience and opinion that exists in a group of adult learners. There will not always be agreement or consensus. The leader may find that living with the questions is more important than finding the right answers. Helping the learner to search for better questions and share personal insights is often more productive than looking for answers.

As beginners in adult Bible study, the learners also bring many insecurities and uncertainties about their ability to participate successfully. The questions and activities in the resource help learners explore the biblical material as it connects with their experiences. One of the goals of this course is to help learners become more confident in their ability to read and understand the Bible. Most adults who participate in this basic Bible course will quickly gain the skills and confidence necessary to participate in a more in-depth level of study as they seek to learn how to respond to their call to follow Jesus.

Needs of adult learners

Adults are motivated to participate in Bible study by a diverse set of interests and questions. Kent L. Johnson, a professor of Christian education, suggests that coping with transitions is the single most common motivating factor (*Developing Skills for Teaching Adults*, Teaching the Faith Participant Guide [Minneapolis: Augsburg Fortress, 1993], 6f). Adults are all, however, seeking enrichment, growth, and ways to make a positive difference in their lives and the lives of others.

Leaders need to recognize the varying needs of the adult learners in their groups. Michael Sack identifies four distinct adult audiences in our churches today. Each generation, according to Sack, has its own identity and needs:

Generation X includes adults who are 16 to 25 years old. They battle low self-esteem and gather in small groups of their peers for support and nurture. They turn to the church for unconditional acceptance and to hear a message of hope.

Busters are 25 to 35 years old. They are firmly grounded and can provide strong leadership for the church. They need relationships, to talk things over with their peers, and to work for a better world.

Boomers are 35 to 50 years old. They look to faith in Christ for a stabilizing influence. They need to discuss meaning, self-definition, and worth.

Older adults are 50 and up. They possess skills and want to do something worthwhile. They need to be appreciated for their experience, insight, and abilities.

This is one way to demonstrate the diversity among adult learners. It is important to recognize that within each of these groups there are individuals who struggle with personal issues. In the course of this study, each individual needs to be heard, respected, and affirmed.

(From *Brain Scan of America* by Michael Sack, copyright © 1995 Michael C. Sack, Cultural Insights, Inc.)

Learning styles

Adult learners have different learning styles. This has to do with how they prefer to encounter and act upon new insights and information. Some adults sit quietly, watching and listening to the group before drawing their own conclusions. Others appreciate the opportunity to do a skit or play a role to express their thoughts and feelings. Some prefer a presentation followed by a question-and-answer period. Others show little interest in group solutions, preferring to act as individuals on practical problems.

To help the leader accommodate the various learning styles of the adult learner, this resource presents two biblical texts—brief segments in the learner book that put the texts into their biblical context—and activities that encourage learning through asking, telling, doing, and imagining. The leader should select activities that guide the participants in a dialogue with the text at all levels—thinking, feeling, intuition, and experience.

Course Introduction

TEN KEY TEACHINGS FROM PAUL'S LETTERS will help people learn something about Paul.

Born Saul of Tarsus, this young man, a highly-educated Jew, rigorously observed the requirements of the Law. Encountering some of the earliest believers in the risen Christ and realizing their threat to Judaism, Saul set out to destroy the Christian church.

But his destruction and persecution were interrupted by an awesome display of God's power (Acts 9:1-22), after which Saul was converted to Christianity, baptized, and renamed Paul. It can be argued that anyone so impassioned with the Law and so confident of one's mission could not have been converted by reason or debate, but only by something as powerful and dramatic as a blinding light. Whatever the truth of that statement, Paul would never be the same person after his Damascus road incident. Theories, doctrines, and ideas are debatable. Not so with experiences. The person with an experience is never at the mercy of someone with an argument. It is imperative that we remember this life-altering experience when we read Paul's carefully-constructed ideas on sin, grace, salvation, and a host of other religious topics. When Paul makes powerful and seemingly all-inclusive statements, remember his life's journey. In one flash of light and three days of contemplation, Paul surrenders his life's philosophy to the message of Jesus Christ. We dare not underestimate the power of this transforming experience.

Saul, now Paul, fortified by the Holy Spirit and fueled by his own passions, begins a series of missionary journeys to establish small churches. Later, Paul would write to some of these congregations or to individuals, offering them advice to specific problems and making observations about God's relationship to them in their situations. These are Paul's letters which we now have as part of the New Testament.

These are real letters, written for a particular reason, people, or occasion. They were often substitutes for a personal visit, or a follow-up encouragement to a previous visit. It is likely that the letters were circulated among other congregations.

Paul writes with both the precision of a defense lawyer (Romans 6) and the grace of a poet (1 Corinthians 13). He chose words carefully, and the grace of God in Jesus Christ is foremost in Paul's writings. Though he never met Jesus in person, no other writer has so influenced the Christian church as Paul. More New Testament writings have been attributed to Paul than any other writer. Some of Paul's letters are the earliest Christian documents we have. The Christian church is deeply indebted to Paul.

Trying to select ten key verses from Paul is something like trying to find the best gems in a field of diamonds. They are everywhere! But the ten selected here constitute a broad range of Paul's theology as well as tell us something about this author and the church he fashioned which we have inherited.

Session 1   The Big Picture (1 Corinthians 12:12-26)
One In Christ (Ephesians 2:19-22)

Session 2   Dying and Rising with Christ (Romans 6:1-5)
The Lord's Supper: "For You"
(1 Corinthians 11:23-26)

Session 3   There Is No Other Gospel (Galatians 1:10-12)
Christ: The Power and Wisdom of God
(1 Corinthians 1:18-25; 2:1-5)

Session 4   Life In the Spirit (Romans 8:1-4)
Christian Freedom (Galatians 5:13-14)

Session 5   God's Comfort (2 Corinthians 1:3-4)
God's Promise (Romans 1:1-4)

Course Objectives

This course will help the learners:
- learn about ten key passages from the Pauline epistles;
- recognize that God's work in the cross and resurrection is a shaping force in the lives of individuals and communities;
- watch for the work of Jesus Christ in their own lives and communities.

① Belonging as One in Christ

The church, through its many members, is but one body.

1 Corinthians 12:12-26 The Big Picture
Ephesians 2:19-22 One in Christ

Gathering

☐ Have name tags and Bibles available. Welcome the learners to this study and introduce yourself. Have the learners introduce themselves by sharing their names and one thing they believe (it can be about anything).

● ● ● ● ● ● ● ● ● ● ● ● ● ● ● ●

1 Corinthians 12:12-26
The Big Picture

Read the Story

☐ Have learners read the passage from 1 Corinthians and reflect on their own personal strengths and weaknesses. Use the "Moment of Solitude" strategy (page 20 of the leader guide).

☐ Recall a time when you felt a group of people were operating like one body.

Expand the Story

☐ Paul compares the church to our physical bodies. Why is this such a good analogy? What does such an analogy as this say about God's regard for all humanity?

☐ In our baptism we are united with every Christian—past, present, and future. Have the learners pair off and discuss the significance of that.

☐ Use the "Think Tank" strategy (page 20 of the leader guide) in response to the following activity. Using Paul's comparison of the church to our physical bodies, how many "parts of the body of Christ" can we think of?

● ● ● ● ● ● ● ● ● ● ● ● ● ● ● ●

Ephesians 2:19-22
One In Christ

Read the Story

☐ Have the learners read the Bible story either aloud or silently.

Expand the Story

☐ Some early Christians thought that in order to be a Christian, you had to be Jewish first. Why would they have thought that?

☐ Divide the learners into groups of two. Have one learner in each group look up Ephesians 2:11-22 and the other Romans 11:13-24. What is the one thought expressed in both passages?

☐ In groups of three, have the learners discuss experiences or ideas that brought about a radical change in the way they look at their world and their place in it. Use the "Teaching Twosome" strategy (page 20 of the leader guide).

Focus the Stories

☐ Have learners create a diagram or picture of their ideal church. Use the "More Heads Are Better Than One" strategy (page 20 of the leader guide).

☐ Have learners think about ways to heal division in a family crisis. Use the "We're In This Together" strategy (page 20 of the leader guide).

Closing

☐ Pray together the prayer on page 10 of the learner book. If you would like, close by singing together a hymn such as "In Christ There Is No East or West."

p. 23 learner k.
p 24 q 25 timeline
p 26. how to read bible
glossary

② A New Life in Christ

We have been set free through Jesus Christ.

Romans 6:1-5 Dying and Rising with Christ
1 Corinthians 11:23-26 The Lord's Supper: "For You"

Gathering

☐ Invite learners to reflect on their pasts and share one thing they'd like to change if they had the opportunity.

●●●●●●●●●●●●●●●●●●●●●●●●

Romans 6:1-5
Dying and Rising with Christ

Read the Story

☐ Have the learners read the passage. Here is Paul, the debater, anticipating the argument that might arise from the previous chapter, where Paul wrote, "But where sin increased, grace abounded all the more" (5:20). What is the argument Paul antici-pates? What is his answer to that argument?

Expand the Story

☐ Have the learners make a list of fables, legends, and myths they can recall. Discuss how many of these stories are dependent upon the promise of a new life for the main character or for the commu-nity. Use the "More Heads Are Better Than One" strategy (page 20 of the leader guide).

☐ This is a complex passage. Paul is referring to sin not only as an offense but as a power. What differ-ence does this make in understanding Paul's con-cept of sin?

☐ Using the "Brainstorm" strategy (page 20 of the leader guide), try to determine what Paul meant by our being baptized into Christ's death.

☐ How does Christ's death and our baptism result in our walking in "newness of life"? How do those two events tie together?

●●●●●●●●●●●●●●●●●●●●●●●●

1 Corinthians 11:23-26
The Lord's Supper: "For You"

Read the Story

☐ Use the "Reading Partners" strategy (page 21 of the leader guide) and have learners read 1 Corinthians 11:23-26. Suggest the following questions: Why does Paul mention this passage at this time? What is he responding to in the previous verses (11:17-22)? How does Paul think this passage will be received?

Expand the Story

☐ Have learners write down on paper several things they would like to be remembered for. Tell them not to put their names on the paper. Collect the papers and read them aloud to the group. Using the "Who's Ready?" strategy (page 21 of the leader guide), find out who the group thinks wrote each list.

☐ Have learners think about what it means to "pro-claim the Lord's death until he comes." Use the "One at a Time" strategy (page 21 of the leader guide) and discuss the answers.

Focus the Stories

☐ Jesus came to earth "for us and for our salvation" we confess in the Nicene Creed, and the meal he prepared is given to each of us. How do salvation, baptism, and Holy Communion connect? What is their significance to one another?

☐ *For you.* Ask learners to comment on what these words mean to them.

☐ Ask the learners to write down a list of things they remember about a loved one. Use the "Moment of Solitude" strategy (page 20 of the leader guide).

Closing

☐ Pray together the prayer on page 18 of the learner book. If you would like, close by singing together a hymn such as "Thy Holy Wings" by Carolina Sandell (translated by Gracia Grindahl) or "For the Bread Which You Have Broken."

Key Words

Grace

Holy Communion

New Covenant

Old covenant

Righteousness

Sin/Transgression

③ Paul's Boldness in Preaching

The power and wisdom of God is expressed in the Gospel of Jesus Christ.

Galatians 1:10-12 There Is No Other Gospel
1 Corinthians 1:18-25; 2:1-5 Christ: The Power and Wisdom of God

Gathering

☐ Have the learners read Galatians 1:10-12 using the "Reading Partners" strategy (page 21 of the leader guide).

● ● ● ● ● ● ● ● ● ● ● ● ● ● ● ● ● ● ●

Galatians 1:10-12
There Is No Other Gospel

Read the Story

☐ Paul is upset as he writes to the Galatians. Read Galatians 1:6-7 to see why. Why do you think Paul was so upset? At least two things were being challenged here. What are they?

Expand the Story

☐ Have learners write an advertisement to your congregation selling Paul as an evangelist or guest preacher based on this text. What are the key terms he uses to "sell" himself in either of these roles? Use the "Wherever Three or Four" strategy (page 21 of the leader guide).

☐ Have the learners share a time when they felt they may have experienced an unexplained event or revelation. Use the "One at a Time" strategy (page 21 of the leader guide).

☐ Paul was concerned that the gospel of Jesus Christ not become adulterated with other doctrines. Does that idea ever concern you in regard to current issues and church politics?

● ● ● ● ● ● ● ● ● ● ● ● ● ● ● ● ● ● ●

1 Corinthians 1:18-25; 2:1-5
Christ: The Power and Wisdom of God

Read the Story

☐ Read the passage together. Allow a 1- or 2-minute period for meditation.

Expand the Story

☐ Invite the learners to tell of a time they acted "on faith." Use the "Each One Share One" strategy (page 21 of the learner guide).

☐ Discuss how the wisdom of God and the wisdom of the world might differ in various situations. When might they be a corollary to each other?

☐ How might you define "God's foolishness" (1:25)? Use the "Brainstorm" strategy (page 20 of the learner guide).

Focus the Stories

☐ How does the gospel play itself out in the Lord's Supper? Should some people be excluded from the Lord's Supper or shall there be requirements for participating in the Supper? Use the "Opinion Poll" strategy (page 21 of the leader guide).

Closing

☐ Pray together the prayer on page 30 of the learner book.

Key Words
Atonement

Gospel

Law

Salvation

4 The Freedom of the Christian

Free indeed! We are free indeed!

Romans 8:1-4 Life in the Spirit
Galatians 5:13-14 Christian Freedom

Gathering

☐ Using the "Each One Share One" strategy (page 21 of the learner guide), have each person name one of his or her favorite hymns and tell why it is their favorite.

● ● ● ● ● ● ● ● ● ● ● ● ● ● ● ● ● ● ●

Romans 8:1-4
Life in the Spirit

Read the Story

☐ What does it mean to be "set free?" Using the "Think Tank" strategy (page 20 of the learner guide), brainstorm on how many ways God has "set us free."

Expand the Story

☐ Have learners think about what it means to live "according to the spirit." Use the "Moment of Solitude" strategy (page 20 of the leader guide).

☐ Have learners read Isaiah 36 using the "Reading Partners" strategy (page 21 of the leader guide). List all the references to newness contained in this text. Use the "Wherever Three or Four" strategy (page 21 of the leader guide).

☐ How would you explain the difference between the "new law in Christ" and the "old law of atonement"? Divide the learners into groups of two and let them use the "Teaching Twosome" strategy (page 20 of the leader guide).

● ● ● ● ● ● ● ● ● ● ● ● ● ● ● ● ● ● ●

Galatians 5:13-14
Christian Freedom

Read the Story

☐ Have the learners read the Galatians passage using the "Reading Partners" strategy (page 21 of the leader guide).

☐ Help the learners memorize this passage by saying each phrase aloud and having them repeat it.

Expand the Story

☐ Have the learners list ways in which they can serve their neighbors in love. Use the "Brainstorm" strategy (page 20 of the leader guide).

☐ Have learners recall acts of love bestowed on them using the "Each One Share One" strategy (page 21 of the leader guide).

☐ Using the "Brainstorm" strategy (page 20 of the leader guide), try to determine what it means to be "called to freedom" (5:13).

Focus the Stories

☐ How is the freedom of the Christian different from anyone else's freedom? What does this "freed state of being" do to us in terms of how we live? Use the "Interview" strategy (page 21 of the leader guide).

Closing

☐ Pray together the prayer on page 38 of the learner book. If you would like, close by singing together a hymn such as "Blest Be the Tie that Binds."

Key Words
Holy Spirit
Justification
Sanctify
Sinful nature

⑤ God as Provider

The presence of God in comfort and promise.

2 Corinthians 1:3-4 God's Comfort
Romans 1:1-4 God's Promise

Gathering

☐ Using the "Each One Share One" strategy (page 21 of the leader guide), have the learners give examples of times when they have received comfort.

● ●

2 Corinthians 1:3-4
God's Comfort

Read the Story

☐ Slowly read aloud the passage to the learners three consecutive times while they quietly meditate on the passage.

Expand the Story

☐ We have a God who "consoles us…so that we may be able to console." We have a God who loves us first that we might love others. We have a God who forgives us in order that we might extend forgiveness to others. What do these attributes of God say about the nature of God?

☐ Have the learners interview one another to find out how they reacted to a situation in which they either needed comfort or were able to give comfort. Use the "Rewrite" strategy (page 21 of the leader guide).

☐ Someone has said, "When you find yourself in the hot waters of life, you can become like an egg: rigid and hard-boiled. Or you can become like a potato: soft and mushy." What determines which one a person becomes? Do you think God might have a preference? Why?

Coffee — in hot water changes the water

● ●

Romans 1:1-4
God's Promise

Read the Story

☐ As you reflect on this text, put yourself in the place of a Roman citizen or a resident of Corinth or Ephesus. How difficult would it be to believe that Jesus was the promised Messiah? What reasons could be given pro or con to support a point of view?

Expand the Story

☐ Have learners reflect on how God might say "no" to us but still keep his promise to us. Use the "Each One Share One" strategy (page 21 of the leader guide).

☐ Dietrich Bonhoeffer, a German theologian of the twentieth century, said, "Trust always exists in the air of a necessary mistrust." How does that statement relate to God's promises? Or even our own? Use the "Wherever Three or Four" strategy (page 21 of the leader guide).

☐ Have the learners reflect on the connection between hope and promise. Use the "Brainstorm" strategy (page 20 of the leader guide).

Focus the Stories

☐ Based on your study of Paul's teachings and your previous knowledge of the scriptures, what assurance could you give to someone who didn't know God's grace that our God is truly a gracious, loving, and merciful God? Is our God a god of abundance or a god of scarcity? What proof can you offer for your opinion? Use either the "Think Tank" or "Brainstorm" strategy (page 20 of the leader guide).

Closing

☐ Pray together the prayer on page 45 of the learner book. If you would like, close by singing together a hymn such as "Lord of all Hopefulness."

⑥ Rejoice in the Lord Always

May the peace of Christ guard your heart and mind.

Philippians 4:4-7   No Need for Anxiety

Gathering

☐ Have the learners memorize Philippians 4:7 by saying the verse and having the learners repeat after you. Then ask the learners to divide into pairs, make the sign of the cross on each other's forehead, and repeat verse 7 in prayer form: "May the peace of God guard your heart and mind in Christ Jesus."

● ● ● ● ● ● ● ● ● ● ● ● ● ● ● ● ● ● ● ●

Philippians 4:4-7
No Need for Anxiety

Read the Story

☐ Ask for learners to volunteer to read aloud one verse apiece from this passage. In this series of brief exhortations, do you see a central idea emerge? Can we count on God? Will God provide for us? Have learners meditate on how God might provide for them right now.

Expand the Story

☐ Ask the learners how they would describe "the peace of God." How does it differ from a worldly peace? Divide the learners into two groups using the "Talk It Out" strategy (page 21 of the leader guide).

☐ Paul exhorts the Philippian believers to let their gentleness be known to everyone. Why is it so important for believers to demonstrate an attitude of gentleness? How does one acquire an attitude of gentleness? Name some people in whom you recognize that characteristic.

●●●●●●●●●●●●●●●●●●●●●●

Focus the Story

☐ Reflect on how this Bible study will affect your spiritual beliefs. Use the "Moment of Solitude" strategy (page 20 of the leader guide).

☐ What main ideas did you derive about God from this study? Use the "Each One Share One" strategy (page 21 of the leader guide).

☐ Divide the learners into two groups and ask each group to write a one-sentence summary of each session's main focus. Allow them to consult their bibles or their learner books if they wish. Share each group's summary statement and formulate one statement out of the two.

Closing

☐ Pray together the prayer on page 45 of the learner book. If you would like, close by singing together a hymn such as "Lord, Keep Us Steadfast in Your Word."

Discussion Strategies

Introduction

The following strategies will help adults learn together, as well as draw on their creativity, their faith, and their experiences. They will also encourage them to take active roles in congregational life by giving them opportunities to work with others toward a common goal.

Moment of Solitude
(Sessions 1, 4, and 6)

Learners work silently in a corner of the room or in separate areas of the building to either read an assignment, master a task, write a report, memorize a section of scripture, or write reflections in a journal. Then learners return to class and share insights from their solitude. This is a somewhat different "discussion" strategy in that sometimes the discussion is not with the class but with God.

The advantage of this strategy is that it cuts down on distractions and helps the learners begin to deal with their personal thoughts and feelings. Allow time for sharing thoughts and insights in the larger group. Learners should share only what they are comfortable having the group know.

Think Tank (Sessions 1, 4, and 5)

Ask the group to brainstorm all possible responses to a given question and list them on chart paper or a chalkboard. They are to share whatever word, thought, or mental image that comes to their minds, no matter how silly the responses may seem to them or others. Do not make or tolerate any judgmental comments.

Teaching Twosome
(Sessions 1 and 4)

Learners do work on their own; then they find a partner and share with that partner. The strategy emphasizes that as individuals learn they also teach, and that you can learn from each other. It is not necessary that reports be made to the entire group.

More Heads Are Better Than One
(Sessions 1 and 2)

A question is asked, and then the learners work together in groups of three or four to reach a consensus and develop a common answer, which is then shared with the larger group. Consensus is reached when all members agree or can, at least, live with the answer offered.

In this strategy, one person in each small group must act as moderator. The moderator makes certain that all members speak and are not interrupted, restates major points of the discussion, helps the group form a consensus statement, makes sure everyone comes to accept the statement through votes or other methods, and shares the group's work with the whole group.

As you use this strategy throughout the course, invite different people to be the moderator. It is helpful to choose those whom you feel will do a good job at this initially so they can serve as good role models, but everyone should have the opportunity to play this role. You can help learners be successful in this role by roaming from group to group, listening in, and offering positive comments or gentle guidance.

We're In This Together
(Session 1)

Have the learners work in pairs, and then combine with another pair to share their work. As leader, move about the room and observe the progress of each group. Have the groups report to the whole group when they are finished. This strategy helps learners build confidence in their ability to work together.

Brainstorm
(Sessions 2, 3, 4, and 5)

This strategy works best when combined with the visuals of a chalkboard or chart paper. Here you might say, for example, "Let's make a list of all the ways that _____." Then invite the learners to respond with whatever ideas come to mind. Write their ideas down on the chalkboard or chart paper as you hear them.

Reading Partners
(Sessions 2, 3, and 4)

Invite learners to pick a reading partner for the six sessions. If you have an uneven number of learners, assign three to one group.

Each reading pair is responsible for reading from the learner book and the Bible as assigned. Each pair can decide for themselves who will read when and how much. (It might happen, for example, that in some pairs one person does all the reading. Ideally, each partner will take a turn.)

Who's Ready? (Session 2)

In this discussion technique, the learners choose for themselves when to respond. You might say, "Let's discuss these questions. Who would like to begin?"

The advantage of this method is that the learners can talk when they are ready. You, however, have the responsibility of making sure each learner responds, and you may have to call on those who don't volunteer.

One at a Time (Session 2)

Call on the learners individually. Direct those not called upon to listen quietly and attentively. Ask the learner who is answering to clarify or elaborate as needed.

In addition to calling on the learners one at a time, you also can take the questions one at a time. That is, you would have each learner answer the first question, then the second, and so on. This strategy gives individual attention to each learner and it proceeds through the questions in a sequential manner.

Wherever Three or Four
(Sessions 3 and 5)

Divide the learners into groups of three or four for the purpose of discussing a question or working cooperatively to complete a poster, collage, or other activity. This is helpful not only for small group work, but it teaches learners that Christ's presence is at work in the smallest groups of two, three, or four.

Each One Share One
(Sessions 3, 4, 5, and 6)

In groups of three or four, the learners take turns sharing thoughts about any question or issue. In doing so,

they need to know that their thoughts and their opinions are valid and will be affirmed. This strategy can be used to build trust levels within the classroom.

Opinion Poll (Session 3)

This strategy challenges the learners to be introspective and expressive. Tell the learners you are conducting an opinion poll. Ask them to imagine a continuum (line) stretched across the room, with the words *Strongly Agree* at one end and the words *Strongly Disagree* at the other end. Poll their opinions on a chosen topic by reading to the learners a list of statements about that topic.

After each statement, ask the learners to take positions along the continuum that match how they feel about the statement. After everyone has taken their places, ask them about their opinions. Discuss the range of opinions and explore the trends shown by the poll.

Interview (Session 4)

Have the learners interview one another or someone outside the group. The purpose is to get each learner to think about the question, and to hear a variety of responses or a new perspective on the question.

Rewrite (Session 5)

Give learners the opportunity to explore the meaning of a specific message or lesson by instructing them to rewrite or tell what they have studied or learned in their own words. Have them work in pairs or small groups. Encourage them to put the information in their own words. Then encourage the learners to exchange and discuss what they've written with another pair or small group. Have them find out if what they've written speaks more clearly than the original message. What points did they miss?

Talk It Out (Session 6)

Divide the learners into two groups. Provide each group with an opposing opinion statement to consider and support. Give each group time to reflect independently on its opinion statement. Provide paper and pencils for those who would like to write down their thoughts. After a couple of minutes, ask each group to present its argument to the large group. Allow time for the learners to respond to each presentation.

Weekly Journal

WRITING IN A JOURNAL may help you focus on the important things you have read and discussed with others. It may also help you clarify what you believe. Use this journal page each week to record your thoughts and questions and put your feelings about what you have learned into words.

Session 1: Belonging as One in Christ

1. What new thought came to me in this session?

2. What is one question I have about these texts?

3. What is my understanding of the church?

Session 2: A New Life in Christ

1. What new thought came to me in this session?

2. What is one question I have about these texts?

3. What is my understanding of sin and grace?

Session 3: Paul's Boldness in Preaching

1. What new thought came to me in this session?

2. What is one question I have about these texts?

3. What is my understanding of the term *gospel*?

Session 4: The Freedom of the Christian

1. What new thought came to me in this session?

2. What is one question I have about these texts?

3. What is my understanding of the work of the Holy Spirit?

Session 5: God as Provider

1. What new thought came to me in this session?

2. What is one question I have about these texts?

3. What is my understanding of the concept of "freedom in Christ?"

Session 6: Rejoice in the Lord Always

1. What new thought came to me in this session?

2. What is one question I have about this text?

3. What is my understanding of the peace of God?

Reflection

TWO WELL-KNOWN PASSAGES from Paul are reproduced here and divided into daily contemplations, each for one week's time. Choose one of the passages and reflect on each verse as you go through the week. Take time to dwell on the verse for each day. You may want to commit these passages to memory.

Romans 8:31-39

Day 1

What then are we to say about these things? If God is for us, who is against us?

Day 2

He who did not withhold his own Son, but gave him up for all of us, will he not with him also give us everything else? Who will bring any charge against God's elect? It is God who justifies.

Day 3

Who is to condemn? It is Christ Jesus, who died, yes, who was raised, who is at the right hand of God, who indeed intercedes for us.

Day 4

Who will separate us from the love of Christ? Will hardship, or distress, or persecution, or famine, or nakedness, or peril, or sword?

Day 5

As it is written, "For your sake we are being killed all day long; we are accounted as sheep to be slaughtered."

Day 6

No, in all these things we are more than conquerors through him who loved us.

Day 7

For I am convinced that neither death, nor life, nor angels, nor rulers, nor things present, nor things to come, nor powers, nor height, nor depth, nor anything else in all creation, will be able to separate us from the love of God in Christ Jesus our Lord.

1 Corinthians 15:50-57

Day 1

What I am saying, brothers and sisters, is this: flesh and blood cannot inherit the kingdom of God, nor does the perishable inherit the imperishable.

Day 2

Listen, I will tell you a mystery! We will not all die, but we will all be changed, in a moment, in the twinkling of an eye, at the last trumpet.

Day 3

For the trumpet will sound, and the dead will be raised imperishable, and we will be changed.

Day 4

For this perishable body must put on imperishability, and this mortal body must put on immortality.

Day 5

When this perishable body puts on imperishability, and this mortal body puts on immortality, then the saying that is written will be fulfilled:

Day 6

"Death has been swallowed up in victory."
"Where, O death, is your victory?
Where, O death, is your sting?"

Day 7

The sting of death is sin, and the power of sin is the law. But thanks be to God, who gives us the victory through our Lord Jesus Christ.

Discipleship

PAUL'S WRITINGS contain many directives on disci-
pling our lives to follow Christ. Two well-known passages illustrate important aspects of discipleship.
Select one of the following passages and reflect on
each day's verses to help you strengthen your discipleship in Christ Jesus. You may want to memorize these
passages.

2 Corinthians 9:6-12

Day 1

The point is this: the one who sows sparingly will
also reap sparingly, and the one who sows bountifully
will also reap bountifully.

Day 2

Each of you must give as you have made up your
mind, not reluctantly or under compulsion, for God
loves a cheerful giver.

Day 3

And God is able to provide you with every blessing
in abundance, so that by always having enough of
everything, you may share abundantly in every good
work.

Day 4

As it is written, "He scatters abroad, he gives to the
poor; his righteousness endures forever."

Day 5

He who supplies seed to the sower and bread for
food will supply and multiply your seed for sowing
and increase the harvest of your righteousness.

Day 6

You will be enriched in every way for your great
generosity, which will produce thanksgiving to God
through us;

Day 7

For the rendering of this ministry not only supplies the needs of the saints but also overflows with
many thanksgivings to God.

1 Corinthians 13:1-8a

Day 1

If I speak in the tongues of mortals and of angels,
but do not have love, I am a noisy gong or a clanging
cymbal.

Day 2

And if I have prophetic powers, and understand all
mysteries and all knowledge, and if I have all faith, so
as to remove mountains, but do not have love, I am
nothing.

Day 3

If I give away all my possessions, and if I hand over
my body so that I may boast, but do not have love, I
gain nothing.

Day 4

Love is patient; love is kind; love is not envious or
boastful or arrogant or rude.

Day 5

It (love) does not insist on its own way; it is not
irritable or resentful;

Day 6

It (love) does not rejoice in wrongdoing, but
rejoices in the truth.

Day 7

It (love) bears all things, believes all things, hopes
all things, endures all things. Love never ends.

Paul's Missionary Journeys

PAUL AND BARNABAS were chosen to spread the gospel westward from the Antioch church. Their first journey took them to Cyprus, Asia Minor, and then back to Antioch in A.D. 45–46.

On Paul's second journey in A.D. 48–51, he headed back to Asia Minor to visit the churches he and Barnabas had founded. He was accompanied by Silas and was later joined by Timothy at Lystra. This journey included stops in Asia, Macedonia (Europe), and Greece before returning to Antioch through Caesarea.

During Paul's third journey in A.D. 52–62, he evangelized at Ephesus for three years (A.D. 53–56). There the temple of the pagan goddess Artemis, or Diana, attracted many worshipers. Enemies at the churches of Galatia and Corinth worked against Paul during this time. The artisans who made shrines for Artemis finally stirred up a riot against Paul and drove him from Ephesus (A.D. 56). From there he traveled to Greece and then back to Miletus, Tyre, Caesarea, and on to Jerusalem. After an arrest, imprisonment, and a stormy voyage to Rome in A.D. 59–60, Paul was once again free to preach and teach about Jesus Christ.

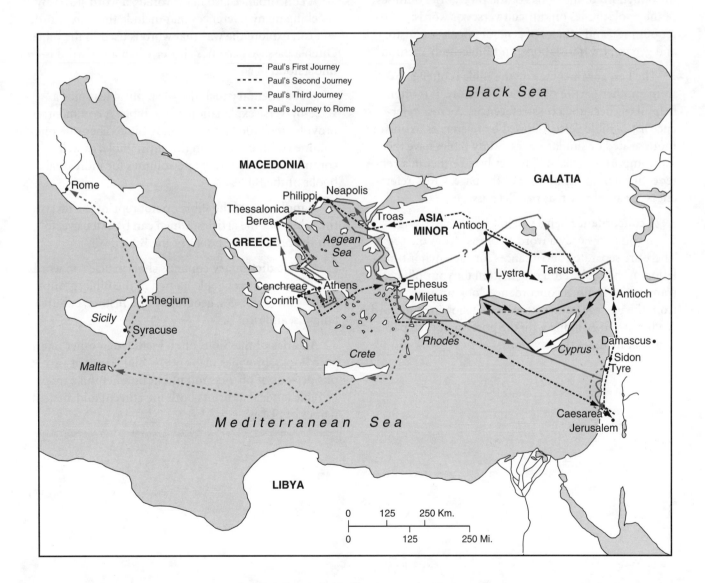

Bible Study Resources

AS YOU READ THE BIBLE, expect to have questions about the text. Also know that exploring the Bible can be a daunting job for anyone. But be assured, too, that there are many excellent references to help a person. Here is an overview of the most common types of helps:

Reference materials, short versions of the materials described below, are printed in the backs of some Bibles. The references are often printed as separate volumes, however, and cover topics more extensively.

An **annotated or study Bible** typically contains introductions to the books of the Bible; brief outlines of the books; notes on difficult verses or words; chapter outlines; and articles of general interest on history and geography, translations, and Bible study methods.

The best commentary on the Bible is often a text from another part of the Bible. Therefore, it is often helpful to check the **cross-references**. A cross-reference lists a Bible verse followed by references to one or more related or similar verses. Study Bibles have the most important cross-references listed either in a center column or at the bottom of the page. Cross-references are also known as parallel passages.

A **concordance** helps you locate a Bible passage when you know only a word or phrase from the verse. There are separate concordances for each major translation of the Bible. Find one written for your Bible's translation. To use a concordance, look up a key word from the passage you want to find. Following the word is a list of verses, along with the portion of each passage that includes the key word.

For example, to find the verse that starts "God so loved the world… ," look up the word *world*. Notice that the Bible verses are listed in the order they appear in the Bible. Scan the verses. After John 3:16 you will find the phrase, "God so loved the *w*." You can look up the passage, explore the surrounding text, and check cross-references.

When you decide which word to look up, choose one that is important in the verse but that is not too common. In this case, for example, you would not look up *God* or *love* because there would be too many references to review easily.

A concordance also helps you do a word study. By checking many references that include the same word, you can explore the way that word is used in the Bible. Often a passage becomes clearer when a key word is understood in a new light.

A **commentary** includes the biblical text plus a verse-by-verse explanation of the Bible. A commentary provides more detail than a study Bible. There are one-volume commentaries on the entire Bible, as well as commentaries with separate volumes for individual books of the Bible.

Handbooks of the Bible do not reprint the text of the Bible, but the articles, which can be extensive, follow the order of the books of the Bible.

A Bible **dictionary** contains short articles on words and topics such as people named in the Bible, groups such as the Pharisees, geography and history, culture, animals, and rituals.

An **atlas** of the Bible, often included in other reference books, provides maps of the Bible lands at various periods of history. You might find helpful a map of Bible lands that prints both the current and ancient names of places.

From *Bible Reading Handbook* by Paul Schuessler, copyright © 1991 Augsburg Fortress.

Bible Bookmarks

1 Cor. 12:12-26
The Big Picture

Almighty God, you sent your Son to proclaim your kingdom and to teach with authority. Anoint us with the power of your Spirit, that we, too, may bring good news to the afflicted, bind up the brokenhearted, and proclaim liberty to the captive. Amen.

© 1978 Lutheran Book of Worship

Ephesians 2:19-22
One In Christ

Almighty God, you show the light of your truth to those in darkness, to lead them into the way of righteousness. Give strength to all who are joined in the family of the Church, so they will resolutely reject what erodes their faith and firmly follow what faith requires. Amen.

© 1978 Lutheran Book of Worship

Romans 6:1-5
Dying and Rising with Christ

O God, you have prepared for those who love you, joys beyond understanding. Pour into our hearts such love for you that, loving you above all things, we may obtain your promises, which exceed all that we can desire; through your Son, Jesus Christ our Lord. Amen.

© 1978 Lutheran Book of Worship

1 Cor. 11:23-26
The Lord's Supper: "For You"

God of all mercy, by your power to heal and to forgive, graciously cleanse us from all sin and make us strong; through your Son, Jesus Christ our Lord, who lives and reigns with you and the Holy Spirit, one God, now and forever. Amen.

© 1978 Lutheran Book of Worship

Galatians 1:10-12
There Is No Other Gospel

God, our maker and redeemer, you have made us a new company of priests to bear witness to the Gospel. Enable us to be faithful to our calling to make known your promises to all the world; through your Son, Jesus Christ our Lord. Amen.

© 1978 Lutheran Book of Worship

1 Cor. 1:18-25; 2:1-5
Christ: The Power and Wisdom of God

Eternal Lord, your kingdom has broken into our troubled world through the life, death, and resurrection of your Son. Help us to hear your Word and obey it, so that we become instruments of your redeeming love; through your Son, Jesus Christ our Lord. Amen.

© 1978 Lutheran Book of Worship

Romans 8:1-4
Life In the Spirit

God, the Father of our Lord Jesus Christ, as you sent upon the disciples the promised gift of the Holy Spirit, look upon your Church and open our hearts to the power of the Spirit. Kindle in us the fire of your love, and strengthen our lives for service in your kingdom. Amen.

© 1978 Lutheran Book of Worship

Galatians 5:13-14
Christian Freedom

Lord God... the battle of good and evil rages within and around us, and our ancient foe tempts us with his deceits and empty promises. Keep us steadfast in your Word and, when we fall, raise us again and restore us through your Son, Jesus Christ our Lord. Amen.

© 1978 Lutheran Book of Worship

2 Corinthians 1:3-4
God's Comfort

Almighty and eternal God, you know our problems and our weaknesses better than we ourselves. In your love and by your power help us in our confusion and, in spite of our weakness, make us firm in faith; through your Son, Jesus Christ our Lord. Amen.

© 1978 Lutheran Book of Worship

Philippians 4:4-7
No Need for Anxiety

Almighty God, you sent your only Son as the Word of life for our eyes to see and our ears to hear. Help us to believe with joy what the Scriptures proclaim, through Jesus Christ our Lord. Amen.

© 1978 Lutheran Book of Worship

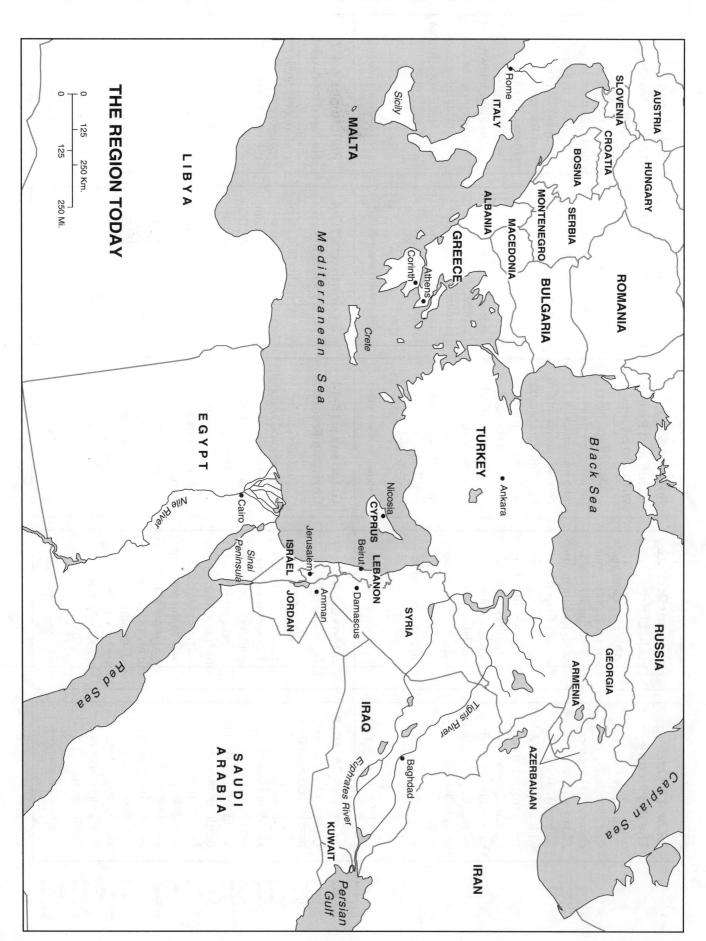

THE REGION TODAY

Scale: 0 — 125 — 250 Km.

0 — 125 — 250 Mi.

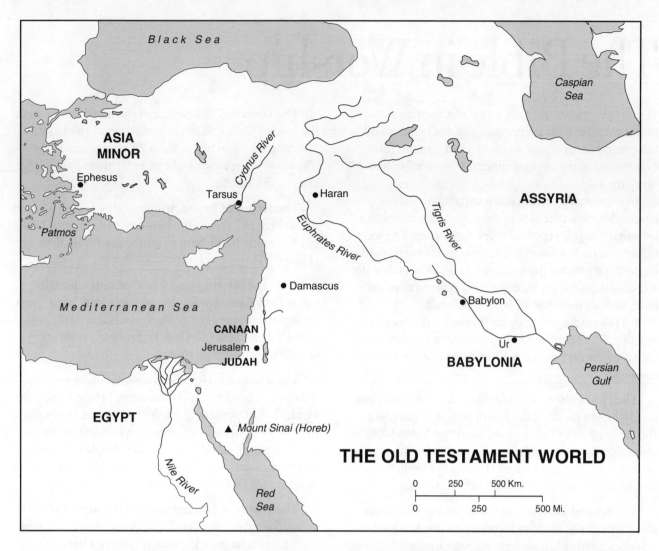

Black Sea

Caspian Sea

ASIA MINOR

Ephesus

Cydnus River

Tarsus

Haran

Tigris River

ASSYRIA

Patmos

Euphrates River

Mediterranean Sea

Damascus

Babylon

Ur

CANAAN

Jerusalem

JUDAH

BABYLONIA

Persian Gulf

EGYPT

▲ *Mount Sinai (Horeb)*

THE OLD TESTAMENT WORLD

Nile River

Red Sea

```
0        250       500 Km.

0        250       500 Mi.
```

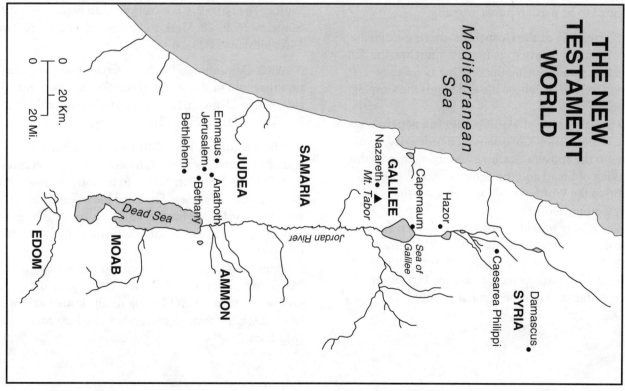

Mediterranean Sea

THE NEW TESTAMENT WORLD

```
0

20 Km.

0

20 Mi.
```

Emmaus

Jerusalem

Bethlehem

Anathoth

Bethany

JUDEA

SAMARIA

Nazareth

Mt. Tabor

GALILEE

Capernaum

Hazor

Dead Sea

Jordan River

Sea of Galilee

Caesarea Philippi

Damascus

SYRIA

EDOM

MOAB

AMMON

The Bible in Worship

THE BIBLE IS AT THE CENTER of Christian worship. From the Bible comes much of the content and the general form of our worship. Each Sunday, for example, as many as three different "lessons" or "readings" are used.

In most mainline Christian congregations, the lessons follow a schedule of Bible readings, called the lectionary, that is repeated every three years. The lectionary, in turn, follows the church year, which begins by preparing us for the birth of Christ; continues with a focus on his suffering, death, and resurrection; and ends with an overview of Jesus' teachings.

All the readings reflect the theme for the Sunday's worship. The sermon, hymns, prayers, and other elements of the service further illuminate the central message.

The First Lesson is usually from the Old Testament, and the main point of the lesson is usually parallel to the main point of the Gospel lesson (see below). Often the congregation responds to this lesson by singing (or reading) a psalm, an ancient Hebrew hymn that was first used in worship in Old Testament times.

The Second Lesson is from one of the New Testament letters, the Book of Hebrews, or the Acts of the Apostles. Many of these writings were originally intended to be used in public worship.

The reading of **the Gospel** has always occupied a place of honor in worship. In most churches, the congregation stands during this reading as a sign of respect for Christ, whose life and words the Gospels relate.

The basic form of worship follows a pattern we can trace to the earliest Christians: "They devoted themselves to the apostles' teaching and fellowship, to the breaking of bread and the prayers" (Acts 2:42). We attend to the Word of God, and we share the Meal, Holy Communion.

The liturgy provides a pattern of spoken and sung texts that give flesh to the basic Word/Meal framework. Many parts of the liturgy are from Scripture. While denominations have a variety of traditions, these examples might be familiar to you:

The Greeting, "The grace of our Lord Jesus Christ, the love of God, and the communion of the Holy Spirit be with you all," is from 2 Corinthians 13:14. The verse is the closing of this letter from Paul to the church in Corinth.

The Hymn of Praise, which begins, "Glory to God in the highest," recalls the hymn the angels sang in the fields outside Bethlehem to announce Jesus' birth (Luke 2:14).

After **the offering** has been received, especially when Holy Communion is not celebrated, some congregations sing several verses from Psalm 51: "Create in me a clean heart, O God, and renew a right spirit within me…" (verses 10-12).

The liturgy for Holy Communion incorporates a number of Bible texts. **The Sanctus,** "Holy, holy, holy Lord, God of pow'r and might," sung near the beginning of this portion of the liturgy, is based on Isaiah 6:3. The prophet Isaiah was in the temple and saw a vision of angels, who sang this hymn of praise. (The word *sanctus* is Latin for "holy.")

The Words of Institution ("In the night in which he was betrayed, our Lord Jesus took bread.… Again, after supper, he took the cup…") do not have a single source. The narrative is a composition based on Matthew 26:26-28; Mark 14:22-25; Luke 22:17-20; and 1 Corinthians 11:23-26.

After Communion has been served, the congregation may join in the **hymn of thanks** that a devout, elderly man, Simeon, sang as he cradled the baby Jesus in his arms (Luke 2:29-32).

One customary **benediction,** or blessing, at the end of the service is from Numbers 6:24-27. God commanded Israel's leader, Aaron, to bless the people with words similar to these: "The Lord bless you and keep you. The Lord make his face shine on you and be gracious to you. The Lord look upon you with favor and give you peace."

Some congregations use another benediction, "Almighty God, Father, Son, and Holy Spirit, bless you now and forever." This blessing recalls Jesus' last words to his disciples before he ascended into heaven (Matthew 28:19).

Using These Resources in Other Settings

TODAY'S NORM for scheduling Christian education opportunities involves flexibility and choices. **Bible Basics for Adults** resources have been designed with this in mind. Each course has been designed for use in six sessions that may vary in length from 45 to 60 minutes. Although this structure will work for many adults, the reality is that today's learners have diverse and unpredictable schedules. Therefore, different options must be available to complete a study.

We learn the biblical message and its importance for our lives in a variety of settings. Corporate worship, devotions, class discussions, retreats, and personal conversations represent some of the ways we learn about the Bible. It is therefore valuable to be open to different possibilities that can help adults begin the journey of studying the Bible as part of their Christian life and faith.

Encourage people to participate in the course by providing alternatives to help learners who cannot attend six weekly sessions.

Mentoring

A study group may want to encourage participants to serve as mentors to one another when someone is absent for a particular session. For example, if Sally is unable to attend a session, Juanita, a fellow learner in the class, could meet with or telephone Sally and share some of the key discussions and learning from the session Sally missed. This way Sally remains connected to the course material, and Juanita enjoys the pleasure of serving a neighbor and reinforcing her own learning at the same time. This experience not only helps Sally and Juanita review biblical material, it also helps Sally remember she is a valued member of the group.

Retreats

Entirely different educational environments can also be explored. A one-day event or an overnight retreat can provide meaningful alternatives to a weekly class schedule. In either case, the course material can be woven together with worship, community-building activities, small group work, games, singing, reflection exercises, and more. All of these possibilities can be developed from recommendations in the leader guide and learner book.

Independent Study

Recognizing that not all adults are willing to study in groups nor able to fit into specific class schedules, another educational format could be an independent study that involves a mentor who helps guide the learning process. This way it is easier to find times when people can meet, discuss the sessions, and learn together. A slight variation of this approach would be to give an individual both the leader guide and learner book and allow him or her to study independently. It would still be good in this scenario to have two or three meetings with another person to reflect upon the insights, questions, concerns, and commitments that emerge from studying the Bible.

Lifelong Learning

Whatever options are explored to help adults begin the journey of lifelong study of the Bible, a primary goal is to learn about the Bible in the context of a community nurturing relationships. This reflects the important principle that building and maintaining caring relationships is integral to Christian education. It reminds us that the Holy Spirit works in our lives through others (1 Corinthians 12:7). The benefit of this goal and principle is the experience of growing in faith through the service, insights, support, and modeling of others.

Glossary

Advocate. One who speaks on behalf of another.

Atonement. The reconciliation of two or more parties.

Baptism. The acceptance of an individual into the family of God.

Church. The people of God, assembled and unassembled.

Comforter. A quality or name ascribed to the Holy Spirit.

Gentile. A person of non-Jewish descent.

Gospel. The good news of the Kingdom of God proclaimed by Jesus Christ.

Grace. The favor and kindness of God freely given.

Holy. Sacred; set apart for God.

Holy Communion. A meal commemorating the forgiveness of our sins.

Holy Spirit. The third person of the godhead who accompanies us in life.

Justification. A one-time act that exonerates the accused. Christ has justified us to God.

Law. The will of God in the form of commands and prohibitions.

Messiah. A king prophesied to come who will save God's people.

New covenant. The restoration of humanity in a new relationship with God.

Old covenant. God's commitment to Israel based on the Law.

Righteousness. Putting or keeping relationships in a right mode.

Salvation. The saving act of God toward God's own people.

Sanctify. To be made holy.

Sin/Transgression. Thoughts, words, and actions of disobedience to God's will.

Sinful nature. The tendency to commit sinful acts.

Key Words
Baptism

Church

Gentile

Holy

Key Words
Grace

Holy Communion

New Covenant

Old covenant

Righteousness

Sin/Transgression

Key Words
Atonement

Gospel

Law

Salvation

Key Words
Holy Spirit

Justification

Sanctify

Sinful nature

Key Words
Advocate

Comforter

Messiah